MUST APPLE

RAE GOUIRAND

EDUCE PRESS

Educe Press
Butte, MT

Published in the United States of America
First Edition, 2018

ISBN: 978-0-9965716-7-8

educepress.com
facebook.com/educepress
twitter.com/educepress

for Naomi

Contents

Acknowledgments

Grateful acknowledgment to the readers and editors of the following publications for publishing these poems, sometimes in earlier versions:

Berkeley Poetry Review: Fig Suite
The California Journal of Poetics: Persimmon
Cider Press Review: Dishes
Conjunctions: Quince Suite
Crab Orchard Review: Behold
Foglifter: Red, November
MARY, A Journal of New Writing: Ghazal With Time
Plainsongs: Brine
Watershed Review: Arils on Velvet, At the Rough Table
Zócalo Public Square: Stanzas to Those Just Arriving

At the Rough Table

There are mornings come each easing
when we almost breathe those dreams—rosemary wreaths

before open windows, felt surfaces rushed
by some more tender breeze. In the turkey feather, in

the deserted hive, her even tone returning
that name first given you, the last wild lace twisting

for its underside. Some daughters stand
in the still of autumn like slant or traveling light.

I have long wished to wake you from it,
to open your ears and then your palms as might

shaking chimes—for I am moved, and
willing to let this day as I have all my others,

to breathe between garlands of chiles
as they dry. It is early yet but the balloons are already

dropping east, goldenrod and marigold, scarlet
and cobalt, copper and maple and umber and thunderclap

and beyond their distant stripes
fog draws unspeakable ink over our valley. I say,

again. I say, unbelievable. At neither point
expecting our words will meet. For now we are locked

as the knots in this wood, this blackberry,
this naked lady, translucent onion, black-eyed susan—

I can gesture to this day only, deliberate
only its roughest seams. Wind on the palm is for many

almost textureless, the cracked husk
finished, not the studded blink of meaning.

I want to stand in the yard
with the year's nearing mess of leaves and press this

to you—to trace the grain of the table
beneath which so many edges are curling, to remember

the ceaselessness that awakens us each
morning, that submits each verse of our living needs.

Dishes

Like cleaning waves of water
with the same: entering

a feeling into a room of feeling.
Admitting to love with

a finite mouth. I want to ask
partnership with all things:

that I should have what is true
before me, that I should see

what I need. Nothing
washes life from itself.

We chase these thoughts until
they go clear, make circles

with sponge on glaze, sense
lather unbinding both

our hands: enter again
the running stream.

Behold

Beans shaking between bent fingers,
my grandfather squints as he snaps the tops off
into the sink, proceeding very slowly,
holding all the beans together in his fist,

the done and undone. I've come to see him
to ask him a question—if you stop seeing
your dreams as you lose your sight, if they become
mere sets of sounds. I have failed to ask.

From his hardened hands I claim the remainders.
He turns toward the tart—the apples have
soaked an hour in a lemon dressing.
His hands wrap around the soft fat halves

and lift them from their syrups to
the light, where he smiles at their progress.
The memorized recipe succeeds: there will be
a fabulous dessert. Each fruit is cut by an easy blade

and smoothed to a gentle fan in the dough,
slice by slice overlapped as sleeping knees.
Once in the oven, it's me who checks the dials,
and soon as it's out the fan turns a satisfied hum.

A sure whiff, and he leaves me leaning
over the grand hot tart like fresh stained glass
unready for hanging, too far from cool. Steaming,
immediate in reddish-peach heat, it's improper

to touch, I know, to breathe too close, and he slips
to his study to write out the ingredients for me.
The new heart hardens and goes a deeper shade.
He makes a sure signature at the bottom, in the dark.

Ghazal With Time

There was a time it felt there was time
for all I longed to be patient for. There was time.

The time around my words was soft
and strong, my question rested. There was time

for all I did not know to do and for all
I needed time for. Patience for all there was. Time

drew its way, assured every unknown.
Here was fine as here, minding there. Was time

not yet something I felt inside? Was
it quiet, quietly spreading there? Was time

my final insurance? My questions
a total sum? Did I trust a sense there was? Time

took my wide open hand and replaced
it with more of the same. Where there was time

I found a reason to believe. In time
there was nothing but nothing. There was time

in me, there was time in being, when
the present was infinite, and there was time

to be infinite again. The one thing
I knew was the only known thing: there was time.

Persimmon

That which returns is sometimes excruciating.
The skin of the persimmons just turning,

seeds stashed in a junk locket, the place you come to
the place you haven't arrived. Every other year,

a friend's tree produces double.
With the first bite, five years one.

I used to think California was expensive.
It's not a surprise anymore, the tree naked but

jeweled—just a treasure, just another kind
of precious junk I didn't make,

that will tarnish from want to keep it.
I love the fruit because the world is bleak

& almost too hard to eat.
I love to be alone. I strain to put a hand

where light has gone, light produced
before I knew the word persimmon, before

I knew the problem love would hand me,
before my hunger was a junk locket

junk chain twisted in my hand.
Can I divine the life of these circles

time makes for us. What is real. What
is not. What is right even when it doesn't fit.

No story is new, but that doesn't mean
we know it: all fruit this strange makes thieves.

Fig Suite

I.

The rip revealing that pink-dark flower,
that latex spilling from open stem—it was not

the fruit that moved me but the wasp
that entered and exited, that made the fig

a thing that could never be promised.
The sky behind us the dull shine of an urn

we sucked resin felt behind teeth. Swallowed
wings dried to sepia, woven with seed.

The wasp & the fig mutual
& unforgivable. My lips

swelled. I wanted salt, water,
more salt. Wanted to tell her what

I found impossible in real time.
We were each looking off at something.

I trusted. Past her, tree branches
twisted out and away. Glue dried

on my front. What redness
at the end, in the center of the hand.

II.

The closer to the trunk, the sweeter
the fruit, but we took even small recesses

for our table. Nubuck to touch, nearly heavy,
the new pulls let their milky-green word,

smelling of some fresh tract. Morning is blue,
afternoon is blue. Everything will change.

III.

One year passed & another gathered:
we stood again under the wide canopy.

The odor her focus: fig-leaf absolute,
herbaceous, mossy, of the wood.

Like cinnamon and urine, the leaves
warm. I swim through my summers

almost wanting to be stung. Reaching
through loose weave for something dark.

IV.

I do not know how we will eat these—
with thick vinegar, or chêvre,

or honey and rough nuts. What
I mean is what will come of it. In the aerosol

of California groves, everything above
hard ground open to the air.

V.

The fig is but one hanging thing. I want
to curl its heart-fan around my hand,

pick wild ones atop a hill, keep
simple time behind wrecked walls.

To stand under an arch & watch ruins
soften, tear something climbing for

the view. The winding path. The vast
sensing. To take something for plain pain.

Many have fallen, grabbed the ground—
under the tree a bed of dried points.

VI.

I imagine my roof cleared & menacing,
my own stone outline walked away from.

Look for what can be taken home
& think only a full pail & the walk.

This year's black missions the largest—
the first wave split, overfull of red stars,

drunk on firmament. Their lingering bristle
travels along palm & arm.

VII.

This autumn, heat everlasting, sacks
of figs before me. Their weight erases

nothing. There is a relief: I
can concentrate on the work, not

think of the self. Keep silent &
watch circles run away with themselves.

VIII.

None can predict how long it might be
before the moment shifts. How late

in the year we'll find wet fruit.
We go into the rains watching those

we can't reach, their skins now
second skins. Leaves go, branches

whiten. What wakes before winter
knows us from year to year, our

shaking hands reaching out
preparing to close.

IX.

Light shifts on all it finds,
offers glimpse of what might come

after this world, this moment's
fruit. Itself settles into

the skins, moves the flesh
toward its sugar, moves

what's ripe toward some version
of wine. We are forgetting

is the refrain
to every feast song I've sung.

X.

Branches gesture to space, know
pieces of air from other pieces, bear

these pluralities without putting forward
facts. If there were a way

to measure the ache beneath the tree,
or love that takes every surface

for itself, perhaps it would look like this:
form extending from form, offering

the world unnamed things. They fatten
fast, green to the grey world.

Perhaps all hungers are grown in waves
and meant to leave us unresolved.

Desire might be endless: reason
& spark enough. It requires

endlessness, and it pulses. It knows
us before we know ourselves.

Arils on Velvet

I am thrust through myself in this dark we take up,
deep-eyed as the red bulb

exploded on its branch. I too am opened.
I too watch it quartered

that gemmed torture of seed. Watch it sieve—
watch the hand separate

hull from garnet. Pray the cuts of these pupils
might find what is sharp—

there are those who will continue to call one
by name. See these pips. To claim

a clear space one need only split. Sometimes it kills
to marry a definitive thrum, those

hundreds of nows. More granular than grenade
or grenadine—you crown

yourself uncounted. Stand in the place none
describes untouched. May each

catch as that candle in scarlet transparency
against the rub of the couch,

leaving no margins, no room for belief. Once
fruit is set it clamors in its chamber

until it bursts. Choose among these those seeds
you will eat. Most are neat

and hold a stain as dark as any history, as any
commandment we'd be stunned to read.

Stanzas to Those Just Arriving

Once in autumn's ease date palm branches
swung over my back, sugars creamed inside their skins—
I'd never have guessed owls would nest in
anything called the *phoenix*, that we'd practice confessions
watching their shapes come and go on the way out
to prey. But night hung beautifully and
time practiced meaningless phrases. These I didn't pick
but pitted for us, amber in their red skins, so syrupy
and rich. Somehow they crystallize both heaviness and light—

across, some grapes, an heirloom kind from which
dessert wines, those spheres on their stems
the fattest obviates. What readiness beckons, what
(I search for the word—) prescience. In each grape
the rooted vine, its milk vein, its expectation.
Its area of defense & the tense of its fear. Against others
it makes its edge in time and light—its terrain comes
of tongue and fit pierced. Each joins and leaves the terroir
as is its vision, weighing its final collection, its ripened
arc. We cannot finish the inscription on the fence, only
these thinning skins. One plunges the harvest to drown the earwigs—

here our pistachios, freed of their reddening husks, dried
on shallow pans on the grass then boiled a bit
in heavily salted water and dried again for splitting. Botanically,
they're drupes, and until ripe the shells pop almost
as bubble wrap, release a scent like the bloom of a citrus—

the walnut is similarly laborious. There at the base
of its visibly grafted trunk one stoops for fallen nuts that have
rolled under bushes, rubs off the hulls which shred
into black bloom before freeing the shell, airdrying
a few days until the kernel is brittle, cracks only later—
so often worms in the nutmeat after all that.
Why you will count only five laid out.

Walking on olives olives split. Sometimes
one just has to work it out over a bucket with lemons
and salt, some knobs of garlic, and a bundle of bay emitting
its eugenol message. The word buttery throws me—
the center I seek is straight green, that quality
they call peppery. A plane taking off. Crows. Forget
what we've said about crows—past the cactus there is
a ranch. Past the ranch a road sign and then
everything narrows, becomes dirt. Every face nicked
with precision to draw its bitterness out. The green
and purple and black all gradations of the same.
Have you ever tasted an olive straight off the tree?
Sometimes it is time to divorce yourself.

From the ziziphus family, the thorny shade tree of the jujube
releases what tastes at summer's end like crisp green
apple and closer to winter like baked apple while transitioning
from glossy to mottled to full purplish-brown. Often
smoked or dried for tea, eaten with coffee or brandied,
I hear a relative is mentioned in the Qu'ran, that in Japan
a style of nightlight is fashioned after them. I usually chop mine
into stuffing where they are overpowered by aromatics,
by onion and celery and mushroom, by the rowdy sugars
in the meal of corn. But aren't they pretty.

On the pickled seckel pears you must allow me a story.
It's always a house up the coast in my stories. Sometimes
accuracy is all we need—part of what I love about these houses
is there's always something waiting. I was the first to arrive
of the three who were convening and there it was, this platter
covered in several kinds of local cheese, honey-spiced nuts,
black pepper crisps, a golden raisin mostarda,
and these perfectly creepy-looking tiny pear things, all
laid out with a hand-carved wooden knife wedged between.
I stood there staring. It was the most definitive thing.
I wanted to put the knife in my mouth and impress
my teeth. There's an etiquette to not digging in,
but the pears were the sole homemade piece and
on the card there was this little heart. I think
they taste like remembering and forgetting. I just used

apple cider vinegar and plain sugar, salt, cinnamon
sticks, star anise, and some cloves. You'll see.

And in the valleys, winding between: a chunk of honey
spilling out of its wax, a crumbling cheese and
a running one, some salted meat, a dense cake of pounded fig
and almond, some grainy mustard, some rosehips
just because they're lovely, the pickled stems of a chard
I pulled, a lone flower clipped from the orange tree,
and a scattering of larger caperberries, calendula petals'
sparks, an unlikely ring of glowing currants
balanced on a bed of mountain sage, a gooseberry husk,
a dish of candied cherries dark in their syrup, a couple
of poached prunes, sourdough sliced neat
though we tear bread in this house—and in that corner
where the eye begins its wandering, please imagine
an invitation to help yourselves voiced by this
gorgeous nasturtium believed to have migrated over
from the neighbors, though we're uncertain.

Briefings

These words again: come into
your body, be your body.

I can be everything but my bones,
which would keep even

if I burned—I yearn to breathe
fat over muscle, flesh over bone, to know

other matters before bone again,
to keep a little distance from ever-pressing

bone. Were I to cite the occasions
on which someone has put in my hands

that intention to inform me
of what it is I would one day need

to know, those would number
few by comparison to the moments

I have laid hand on what shakes
as I shake reaching, seems

almost to resist my urge to break
form and take something

no one has laid in hand
as given. That stretch beyond the line

shines. This distress, contention, sense
of lack or wrath—I rival nothing

in the field. I accept the field,
its issue. I take the field for

what glows—some impossible focus
that won't be quoted or thrown.

Brine

In late fall my friend arrives, tear-streaked,
her bags tightly packed, her language

shaken. We make soup for each other,
take out pictures from other years,

walk through bookstores recommending
titles. In days she crosses oceans again

to the country where she lives now and
will have it done. There is a crumpled weight

to the blue above our canopy, & bruises
on most of the olives we pick. We take

both large and small all afternoon, until
the light is gone. In evening, we nick each

with a paring blade, and sort them
between us: those going to salt, those not.

Quince Suite

I.

These are not the market gods of last fall, those wrong moons
in their crate by the bay. Nor those shared by the first friend

who whispered her tree. These came by my hand, from that park
across town. Now they litter my counter, insistent scent

of wood and mead— autumn fruit, forbidden fruit. Steroidal,
bruised. In some spots burned. Golden and mature,

smooth to fingertip. Nearly as hard as the blade I use to halve them,
split the seedcluster center. For generosity and loyalty,

cut after cut, pushing at something guarding. Honey apple, elephant
apple, sparrow apple, golden apple. Must apple.

I stand in the rest of the world as though it is a mist. My board
in skins, the group like a sentence. In places where

they're not such a rare find, boys throw bitten ones into
the sea for sweetening. In the pot they go to gold,

then coral, rose, increasingly flowery, increasingly themselves.
I move the spoon through, face hot. When winter comes,

there will be enough, so thick it sticks, the smell to the walls:
honeysuckle and rosewater and cardamom, flesh near red.

Perhaps they know the mouth. Perhaps they lack our secrecy,
boast their own unsaid thing. What is there best so given?

II.

I know only to pick them when they come, to put them to something
I would myself want. Each year the fattening above the side

18

of someone's house, the black flakes of branch as I pull one by one.
The floral air & the thorns, the flush & the pot heavy. I want

to grant it. In gratitude, in demand. To push toward you now through
open air and measured patience the oldest promise one can make.

III.

There are nights in early dark, the window cold
square behind the sink, when the hands must cleave with biggest knife

the hardest fruit, the fruit that's stone
against wood that's cut too, the fruit on it recognizing

its arc, its father and mother and water
and brother the sky, the sky gone dark, the sky held tight

in the mind of the hand, the mind of the hand
bearing the knife that's heavier than hand, the thing we use,

the thing we recognize as having use, something
to reach for, to bring to what we want, to what we enter into, or enter

into us. The quince is dry, the music lush, the organs
hard and loud. The floor beneath the feet hard. The glass hard,

the breath full of edge. What can be separated
from what. This is the stuff of tears when they come—we know

our branch. We are on the wood. We are under
the knife. Thank god for death, for life. On nights so soaked

quince go red for those stones. Those
who have died. New love and the line. Thank god for night.

For the hum that pulls back into
corners as we close. I gather skins in my hands. There is nothing

not gathering. I know devotion. I hurt
and heal. There is so much beneath the deep. The loving animal

on whose back I rest cannot
keep me from feeling as alive as that lightbulb keeping lit—

IV.

I gather language.
Deciduous, dulce, multi-stemmed, many-seeded,

that exfoliating bark
on those twisted, rangy branches that gnarl

with age and grow into
contorted shapes and eventually require buttressing

during their period of
senescence, which is long. Those roots shallow,

girdled. The pome yellow
and vulnerable to the apple maggot and its cycle

whole: spring flower,
autumn color, winter-bare branches that entwine

dramatically. A dense grey-
white pubescence covering the leaves, buds, and fruit,

the flowers large and solitary,
of course, developing on new shoots in spring

and perfect. The seeds
resemble apple-pips, packed dark in the mucilage

of the seedcoats. Some
of the fruit is almost handsome, the rest wooly

until mature, harsh until it's not,
knobby, maybe mottled or sun-browned

or bletted—it bruises surprisingly
once softened by frost. Both humble and

20

exhibitionist, it precedes itself
in its fragrance. Rub off downy fuzz with soft cloth.

Woody, spongy, hard
to cut. But as everything is by heat, as everything

is accelerated—a spicier
dimension erupts, a wild fragrance, some

kind of musk, a headiness,
an aroma of pineapple and pear, guava and vanilla—

ancient traders claimed one
would turn a caravan. Out in front of itself

before anything is next:
the oldest fruits have always said next.

And cooked—deep apricot
then translucent rose, like flowers and honey

have spoken all their lives
then stopped abrupt. In the pot, the flesh

softens, just goes
gorgeous, pinkish. Why is there no verb

for goes translucent? This
moves you; the result beginning

to resemble what you
know and sense and feel into—

V.

But we cannot talk about some grief.
We talk about remembrance, but not death.

We talk about eternity, but not
digestion. We use the language of savoring

but are unable to realize our own
passing, are unable to face our own infinities. The trees

thrive. Some say for thirty years,
others for hundreds. Train with an open center.

Self-reliant, they self-fertilize
and grow wild on the edges of neglected properties

from their own seed. A source.
Important. As real as any other fact that sticks.

Some things live in the waves,
like depth. Depth ever unmistakable. I too wish

to be escorted home. I too begin
more humble. I mean I inherit mostly myself

and my ways of weathering.
I was born in November, a few days in, just past

the tipping point between
exhausted radiance and absolution. Why birth—

why autumn—we go
unmatched otherwise, our whole lives.

Some fruit taps an ancient us,
a memory of emblems. What does this mean

do you remember. Can you
feel it, this proof of this impossible life.

VI.

I wish my own contradictions,
now that I am older, now that I am old enough,

wish them not to resolve each other
until I am neater but to render each other more

impossibly real, until
I am realer, until I am absolutely with this

moment of my life, and with
all the moments that have delivered life into me

and keep delivering life into me.
Anyone who has walked deep into woods

to find a tree has understood
they know nothing of history, that the miracle

is not people but absence,
that the miracle is not forgiveness but evidence,

that the miracle is not anything
other than life remembering itself again. There are

seventeen small seeds inside
the one I have saved to cut last. If I had no

other concerns I would
devote myself to planting every last one in places

they are theoretically not
supposed to survive and die knowing they probably

would, for far longer than I,
in the generous soil and climate of California.

VII.

Native to Caucasus, that mountainous pass between
the Caspian and Black seas, the Greeks called them *strythion*,

the Romans melimelum. Other names ring: *coines, coing,*
Cydonian apple, elephant apple, *maja pahit, ma-tum, quitte, vilvam.*

The quince of Song of Solomon? Probable in the Garden
of Eden and Aphrodite's hand. And those cultivars: Aromatnaya,

Bereczki, Champion, Cooke's Jumbo, Dwarf Orange,
Gamboa, Iranian, Isfahan, Le Bourgeaut, Lescovacz, Ludovic,

Maliformia, Meeches Prolific, Morava, Orange (Apple),
Perfume, Pineapple, Portugal (Lusitanica), Shams, Siebosa,

Smyrna, Van Deman, Vrajna. So much weight to them.
Medieval cooks thought quince the most useful of the fruits.

VIII.

Of what use to Joan of Arc was that small wooden box
of rare confections usually presented to French royalty?

Shaped from the clear goo that results boiling quince juice
and sugar, those little figures of flowers and animals

must have been a difficult gift marking the moment
she arrived in Orleans to liberate the French. I imagine

I'd have begged a land grant, like the Texan who
(in the 1850s) put the first quince in the ground west

of Virginia. From England to Massachusetts they came
by seed request, 1629. See colonial trees, 1720. I might

have said you can keep the *Cotignac d'Orleans*—my eyes
are fixed. And besides, once you've rubbed off that fur

the fruit comes wrapped in, you might read far more
stirring stars beneath. Slice into crescents, press off

the edge of the board to watch their eclipse scatter.
On the tree it births a shadow I swear weighs more

even though it twinkles, that chartreusey demand hanging
amid flaking bark and blighted leaves. Infinitely brighter

than its surroundings. I am so rarely moved but I am
moved. The floor of my thinking is leafed in the dry heat.

IX.

I will find myself beside myself.
I will reach over and over

and sever it from its hold. The fruit
a stress, the stress of the tree,

its feature. When I sever it
it will throw bark in my eye but

I still believe we are meant
to touch it.

X.

The roots of *must* spread wildly—
there is the sense of indispensible, as in must-read.

And of fresh, literally wet. An entry
having something to do with moldiness. And

a side note on male elephant frenzy,
from the Persian word for intoxicated. Also

to have room to, to be able to.
This sticks. Might

must have anything to do with
mustard, which blossoms in the winter here?

I read something about needs,
about the etymology of necessity, from

the Old English, about necessity
as an adverb reinforcing must. Muster, later.

Quince itself begets *meli*, honey. (O Melissa.)
Holds to *malic*. Words invoking preserves

made from tree fruit.
Is fruit by virtue virtuous?

Fruity people are willing to oblige.
Where I say people I mean

people mean women and girls.
Fruitcake for lunatic. Lunatic

for moon-bent. So many nights
are utterly fruitless minus the silence.

XI.

Before the tapesty of the unicorn in captivity
the quince is what I see—no red world

spinning internally, arils beckoning.
Woven in to the wool and the silk and the silver

and the gilt: the oldest fruit. No one
can explain these tapestries; their symbols are

too incredible to summarize. The beast
does not appear unhappy behind his fence, chained

to that tree. Wild orchids and thistles
and violets surround: what I

take away is the powering joy of all life flowing
through its means towards its fulfillment.

Those yellows from weld, reds from madder,
blues from woad—all plants that lived

in the late medieval their hues still distinct.
What is living. In this episode, no

humans pursue the animal; the animal pursues
its solitude. We do not actually require

one another to realize our roles, or require
our roles. We may be seen from a distance—

mysterious initials may even elide in the air
like a consideration speaking itself.

Is the unicorn always in the center of the field?
That horn single and unbelievable. I don't

know that ignorance and allegory are separate
given how fiercely we hold on to each.

XII.

What is our history? What story
after winter turns? If we remembered

all we had ever eaten, would we
realize hunger? Is anything as real

as consideration, as this feeling
of dizziness? The hunt will take place

within a garden that is closed, but
captivity is open, or nearly.

Living things model themselves
whether we can tell symbol from real—

I can't stop wondering how
this stillness relates to being tethered,

specifically, to a tree. And feeling
the density of my own consideration

on the edges of the world in which
I am standing—

Bay Laurels

Leave whole
for the interval before

solids render softer—
bitters sharpen over the hour

and that is needed
for the evening.

Gold is a constant here
half the year or more—

nearly menthol in the morning
rarer than that pepper

one breathes daylong.
We are no one's daughters

now punish only ourselves
at turns—I can walk forever

glint square in my chest
sounding animal sound

as another arrow finds me.
Let me keep such lust—

if I fall from myself
let my own evidence bend

under glass, my oils
gone radical as time bent,

as things curved around
to story themselves.

I am that point
sharper in the mouth

than you'd expect ending
what you may have

been saying—piercing or defining
like anything retold.

Red, November

Leaves clear from the persimmons
as though their fruits swell first

to be illuminated. You wait for trees
to redden where they rarely do,

find minor glints. Nothing is
more generous than the change

of sun over us: setting on water,
replacing our exchange, the whole

story. Stars drop. We are taught
it is a sin to be extravagant, whole

of heart, to flush with our own want
of the world. That kinds of love

are best quieted. A friend's letter
describes an orange room, the choice

to touch something untouched.
Some suffer what they don't, collect

nameless values in present hands.
These our choices at the turn.

Think nothing of giving too much
to what we know as surface—

next year the trees will fruit
half this count; we'll remember

or we won't. Each ache will blaze
the same. Waving branches

direct all these hatched shadows,
suggest many forms day to day.

30

Broth

My oldest friend sits at the table
left to her by her grandmother & describes

the menu she plans for her parents
on Thanksgiving: no gloating

stuffed bird, no glazing of roots.
She wants a roast, just à point,

and some turnips, and a soup—
no, a broth. Something radiant and hot,

given from scraps. When we were small,
we ripped our bread to soak up

the last at dusk, shared our hungers
evenly, doubled over those bowls

until another had settled
we both were done. Each year since

the face of hunger has appeared
before us more precise, our language

for it hungering too—still
that last gleam flashes beneath

all our certain decisions: lucent
and spare, salted, perfect.

Poem in Which the Cold-Hardy Satsumas Fall

From the higher split of the tree
she picked & rolled, those mandarins' drops

slowed by limbs, almost broken, as slow as
it was cold. What exact handling: you felt each land

delicate inside its own pillow. Easy oily faces
loose upon their fruit. Pieces of

her voice too: *There's more. On your right*
and permission: out of fog, ginger-clear on grey,

vivid tint breaking through mist—an eclipse
reversed. The fruit was sour, still just under, but

we wanted this gleaning before we lost out—
the tongue can always find frost.

We stuffed some too-full bags, carried by the task
the way we carry the first person into

most things. So much glows
against flashlight beam, night fog, cloth pocket:

every gesture of the hands dragging branch, branch
combing out a pleural space: every filling

of the lung for the twinge of those slits.
O, ribs: I miss that space,

the way citrus ached every day
over or under-sweet—stabbing, in the hand,

that squat familiar something to squint at.
Where does such belief come from,

that we will last if we live? What promise,
the newly cleared air that released their shapes.

Made in United States
North Haven, CT
22 October 2025